TAMING AND TRAINING AMAZON PARROTS
KW-039

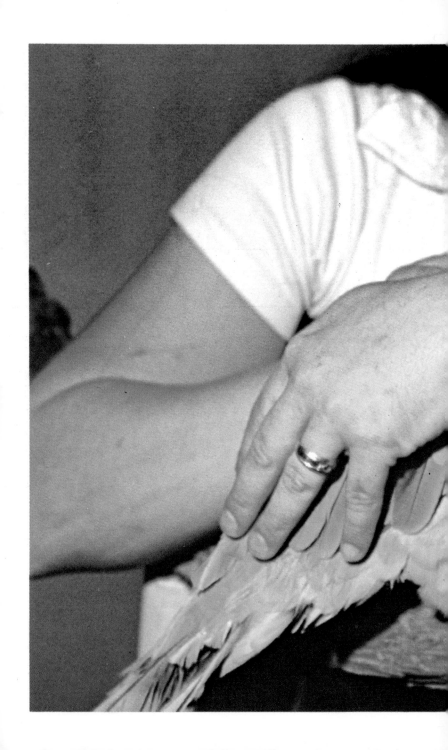

Contents

Title page: Amazon parrots are fascinating, intelligent birds that make wonderful pets.

Overleaf: The author, Risa Teitler, gives her pet Amazon a sufficient amount of love and attention and is rewarded with a delightful, gentle bird.

Photographers: Tom Angermayer, Dr. Herbert R. Axelrod, Cliff Bickford, Tom Caravaglia, Isabelle Francais, Ralph Kaehler, Max Mills, Dr. E. J. Mulawka, K. T. Nemuras, Stefan Norberg and Anders Hansson, Vincent Serbin, Louise Van Der Meid, Vogelpark Walsrode.

© Copyright 1989 by TFH Publications Inc.

Distributed in the UNITED STATES by T.F.H. Publications, Inc., One T.F.H. Plaza, Neptune City, NJ 07753; in CANADA to the Pet Trade by H & L Pet Supplies Inc., 27 Kingston Crescent, Kitchener, Ontario N2B 2T6; Rolf C. Hagen Ltd., 3225 Sartelon Street, Montreal 382 Quebec; in CANADA to the Book Trade by Macmillan of Canada (A Division of Canada Publishing Corporation), 164 Commander Boulevard, Agincourt, Ontario M1S 3C7; in ENGLAND by T.F.H. Publications Limited, Cliveden House/Priors Way/Bray, Maidenhead, Berkshire SL6 2HP, England; in AUSTRALIA AND THE SOUTH PACIFIC by T.F.H. (Australia) Pty. Ltd., Box 149, Brookvale 2100 N.S.W., Australia; in NEW ZEALAND by Ross Haines & Son, Ltd., 18 Monmouth Street, Grey Lynn, Auckland 2, New Zealand; in SINGAPORE AND MALAYSIA by MPH Distributors (S) Pte., Ltd., 601 Sims Drive, #03/07/21, Singapore 1438; in the PHILIPPINES by Bio-Research, 5 Lippay Street, San Lorenzo Village, Makati Rizal; in SOUTH AFRICA by Multipet Pty. Ltd., 30 Turners Avenue, Durban 4001. Published by T.F.H. Publications, Inc. Manufactured in the United States of America by T.F.H. Publications, Inc.

TAMING AND TRAINING AMAZON PARROTS

RISA TEITLER
PROFESSIONAL TRAINER

Opposite: *An Amazon may become upset if teased or mistreated. The author exhibits gentle handling and proper attention. This bird is affectionate, tame, and well adjusted.* **Above:** *The author is shown here with two of the parrot species she considers eminently trainable—a young Amazon parrot and a young African grey.*

Introduction

Amazon parrots are among the most popular of all caged household birds. They are excellent mimics, duplicating the human voice with exactitude. They are individuals with definite personality. Amazons are long-lived birds with a life expectancy of 30 to 50 years. It is hoped that new owners of Amazon parrots can use the information provided in this book to help tame and properly care for captive Amazons. Information on advanced training is given, but the emphasis was intentionally on how to tame the parrot. Most people—at least those who haven't had any experience with birds—don't think of Amazon parrots as being different from other parrots, and they don't differentiate between the many species and subspecies of Amazons either; to the unknowing they're all just parrots. But Amazon parrots are different from other parrots in many ways, not the least of which is their adaptability to taming and training.

Amazon parrots are basically green-plumaged birds with contrasting colors on the nape, crown, face and flight feathers. All are New World parrots, inhabiting a wide range over Mexico, South America and the Caribbean. The most common Amazons in captivity are the Mexican and South American birds, so the text will mention them more often than the Caribbean birds.

Size varies greatly, from about 10 inches to 16 inches in length. The torso is broad, the tail short. The wings are designed for quick take-offs, not gliding flights. The bill is made of hardened keratin and may be black, gray or beige. The feet and legs may be black, gray, beige, yellow or two-toned. Amazons have four-toed feet, two toes pointing to the front and two to the rear.

Life expectancy of the Amazons, like other members of the parrot family, is lengthy, from 30 to 50 years. Some individuals may live even longer. Amazons adapt well to captive life as both single pets or aviary birds. When handled properly, a pet Amazon can become very affectionate. The majority will acquire speech if given regular lessons and some develop extensive verbal and musical repertoires. Intelligence varies among individuals, but most are very clever. With training, they can learn to perform a number of tricks. Disposition is affected by both natural tendencies and the environment. If an Amazon is ignored or teased he can develop

Opposite: *A pair of beautiful Amazon parrots. Amazon parrots have a long life expectancy; therefore, the prospective owner must plan for the arrival of a long-term pet.*

Above: *As gentle as an Amazon may be, it can sometimes be unpredictable. Individual birds have different temperaments.* **Opposite:** *Intelligent, alert, and curious, Amazon parrots have long been known and appreciated as pets.*

into a nasty bird, but if given an adequate amount of attention and love an Amazon can become a very gentle bird. These birds often attach themselves to one or two people and can become jealous if they feel that their relationship with the favorite person is threatened.

The bird caught in the wild may be nervous when you first bring him home, but most Amazons are steady and adjust to change readily. Most young birds are not aggressive, but older birds may be. For this reason it is best to begin with a fairly young bird, one under five years of age, if you intend to tame him. Birds one year and under are extremely desirable for taming and training. The Amazons are reproductively mature at approximately four to five years of age. An Amazon that is older than ten is usually much more difficult to tame and should be approached carefully, for his bite can be very painful. A shy,

When shopping for an Amazon parrot, it is best to look for a young bird. These birds are usually easier to tame and train than are older Amazons.

Before a pet Amazon is completely hand tame, it is best to keep the bird secluded from other birds, as their presence may be distracting.

timid Amazon is rare compared to an outgoing, well adjusted bird. Because they can have very flashy tempers, going from gentle to angry without warning, the Amazons should never be given to children as pets. Even the hand-fed baby can grow up to be an unpredictable adult bird, so always supervise interaction between your Amazon and your child.

Although it is very difficult to judge the age of Amazon parrots, there are a few indications worth mentioning. The plumage of very young birds lacks the sheen of mature birds. Poor plumage does not indicate youth as some dealers will tell you, so be aware. The scales of the feet and legs are smoother on young parrots than on older birds. The white eye ring is more prominent on older birds. Young parrots have very smooth

Above: *A roomy metal cage is an essential for every pet bird. The cage pictured here is too small for the average Amazon, although it is fine for a cockatiel.* **Opposite:** *Even within a seemingly safe cage, your pet bird should always be guarded against other pets.*

eye rings while older birds have eye rings that stand out from the face.

Many varieties of Amazons undergo color changes as they mature. For example, a very young yellow-nape has absolutely no yellow on the nape. Young blue-fronts and double yellow-heads do not have extensive yellow areas on the throat, face and head as they will in adulthood. Other Amazon parrots undergo similar color changes as they mature. Educate yourself before you buy the bird to know exactly what you are buying.

ENVIRONMENTS

A suitable environment is necessary for single pet, aviary breeder and display bird. Some Amazons even become "working" birds, living in a small shop or office. The pet bird should be housed in a metal cage with dimensions no smaller than 20 inches square and 30 inches high. For the tame pet a sturdy bird stand is a part of a good environment. Perches should be no smaller than one inch in diameter. Natural wood perches for both the cage and stand are the best that you can provide. The feet and claws stay in better shape on natural wood.

Parrots are usually hardy birds, but if their cages or stands are placed in drafty or very hot places their health may be undermined. Don't place the bird in direct sunlight or you may dehydrate him. The kitchen is a poor place for the cage because temperatures fluctuate. The housepet thrives best in the room where the family spends most of its recreational time. With the family members around him, the Amazon benefits from attention and activity. Keep the cage away from the door. In cold climates make sure not to place the bird near radiators or gasburning heaters. In warm climates keep him away from air conditioning vents. Temperatures that are comfortable for you are fine for the Amazon. Cold weather does not bother a healthy bird, for the plumage provides excellent insulation from the cold. Indoors, the Amazon lives through the winter as you do, perhaps preferring warmer weather, but well able to take the cold.

In summer, you may keep your pet on a screened patio, but in winter it is best to bring him into the house. Aviary birds that remain outdoors all year round must be given ample shelter from the elements. Outdoor aviaries should be constructed of metal; Amazons will chew through wood and escape. Welded wire, obtainable at the hardware store or lumber yard, comes in many gauges and mesh sizes. Mesh should be no larger than 1 x 2 inches since smaller mesh helps control the entry of rodents and other pests. Whenever birds are

If you plan to keep a number of birds together, be sure that they have plenty of room and that they are provided with enough perches.

housed outdoors, the problem of rodents eating up the birds' rations must be dealt with. The best solution is to use a floor of poured concrete and a small wire mesh. Earthen floors are easily traversed by rodents and are also more difficult to clean. Outdoor aviaries must have adequate shelter and be shaded from direct sunlight.

The book *Building an Aviary* by C. Naether and Dr. M.M. Vriends is an excellent text for people who want to build a backyard aviary. Breeding experiments are best conducted in the outdoor situation. Breeding boxes must be constructed of hard wood and be sheltered from rain and wind. The size of the box depends upon the size of the aviary residents. The grandfather clock style of nesting box is accepted by many varieties of Amazons, including the double yellow-head, blue-fronted and yellow-crowned. Nest boxes should measure 5 feet high and 2 to 2½ feet in width. Entrance holes 4-6 inches in diameter, depending on the size of the

Above: *A tame bird can enjoy the freedom of an open perch as long as it is adequately supervised. It is not wise, however, to take your Amazon outdoors for long periods of time.* **Opposite:** *The beak of an Amazon parrot is made of hardened keratin and can be a formidable weapon.*

parrots, should be placed approximately six inches from the top of the box. Although the Amazons may breed successfully in smaller nest boxes, a larger box should be provided if possible. Use wood shavings to fill the inside of the nests to within one foot of the entrance hole.

Display birds should be housed in an aviary constructed of metal, with dimensions no smaller than 4 feet high, 4 feet wide and 5 feet long. Obviously only three or at most four Amazons would be comfortable in a 4 x 4 foot aviary, so take the number of expected residents into consideration when designing the display cage. Use

natural wood branches for perches or provide dowels with a variety of diameters. Different grips are important in keeping the feet well conditioned. Display birds should not be kept up all night by artificial lighting or social activity. The same is true for the single pet. Amazons must be allowed to stick to the natural routine of rising with the sun and roosting at dusk to remain healthy. One cause of continual heavy molting may be the artificial extension of waking hours. This does not mean that pet birds must go to sleep at dusk every night, but only that we shouldn't keep them up into the wee hours of the morning. Night-

Natural branches make wonderful perches as long as they have not been treated with chemicals of any kind.

Before placing two or more birds together in the same area, be sure they will be compatible.

lights are useful for all birds to keep them from banging into the sides of the cage if something startles them at night. Keep the night-light very dim. Blue or green night-lights can provide adequate light without disturbing roosting birds.

Store or office birds should be kept out of public traffic during business hours. People should be able to see but not touch the parrot. Some Amazons do well on an open perch as long as they are protected from being bumped into by strangers. These birds should not be confined to the open perch 24 hours a day, or they will not get enough exercise. Parrots love to climb around, and the cage is a perfect playground. Working birds should also have a secure place to sleep at night; the cage is more secure than an open perch.

Above: *The feet and claws of the Amazon are kept in shape as the bird grips the perch. Perches for an Amazon should be no less than one inch in diameter.* **Opposite:** *A tame Amazon sits calmly on Ruth Hanessian's arm.*

Buying Your Amazon Parrot

SOURCES FROM WHICH TO BUY

Most Amazon parrots are purchased from a retail pet shop. The retailer may cage the Amazons individually or a few to a cage. Parrots are most easily observed in individual cages. Look for a retailer that displays his birds well and provides a rich diet. The shop should be clean and the cage bottoms changed daily. Feed and water cups should be kept clean and feed and water fresh. Look at both the bird and the cage. If the water is obviously dirty from the day before and the feed unchanged, look for a different retailer. The shop should have a supply of adequate parrot cages and accessories. Many pet shops carry high quality feed for parrots and the important vitamin and mineral supplements that you must give the bird. A well supplied pet shop offers written material on the type of parrot that it has for sale. Literature is often the pet buyers' best guide for feeding and maintaining the bird properly. A good retail store can answer your questions or obtain information from other sources. They can often provide the name of a veterinarian that treats birds. Many pet shops sell non-prescription drugs and preparations for use with parrots, but always seek advice from a knowledgeable person regarding your pet bird's health.

You may be able to locate a breeder of Amazons, but this is unlikely. Breeding Amazons is a difficult undertaking at best. However, if you do know of either a local breeder or one in a nearby state, it is worth the trip to see what he has to offer. Be certain that the out-of-state breeder is not selling you imported birds as domestically hatched. In addition to the retail pet shops, some breeders offer hand-reared parrots. These are by far the best candidates for taming and training. Usually the hand-raised parrots cost more, but the birds are worth more.

Sometimes you get an Amazon that has been someone else's pet. These birds are often untamed, confined to the cage. If the bird is in good health, take it. With older parrots be prepared to spend a great deal of time in the taming process. Sometimes people buy Amazons and resell them when they are unable to tame the bird. Again, if the bird is in good health, buy it. Don't pay a premium price for a parrot that someone else has bought and failed with, but be

Opposite: *Be sure to purchase a bird with bright eyes, shiny plumage, and an active, alert demeanor.*

Opposite: *This Amazon is a fine example of the type of alert, healthy bird one should seek for a pet.* **Above:** *Although it might appear that this bird is biting, it is not. It is simply using its bill to help maintain its balance on the arm.*

reasonable in making an offer.

Some people travel to Mexico and South America and buy a parrot, expecting to bring it home with them. Years ago this was not uncommon. These days, however, you must abide by the law that regulates the importation of parrots. You must have documents to prove the parrot's good health, origin, amount of time in your possession, and destination. No more than two parrots can be brought into the United States per family. Many South American countries demand additional documents before you can leave their country with a parrot. If you plan to bring a pet parrot home from a foreign country as a souvenir of your vacation, be sure that you have followed the procedures exactly.

Write to the Department of Agriculture for information pertaining to bringing parrots into the country as an individual.

The wholesale outlet usually can offer Amazon parrots at a lower price than the retailer. Many will not sell single birds to the public as their business is in quantity sales. Their parrots are not caged for easy viewing. The usual setup is many birds to a single cage. The inexperienced buyer has a hard time trying to choose a good parrot out of a large group. The wholesale employees have no time to educate the buyer. For these reasons and others, it is best to buy your pet Amazon from a clean, reputable retail store.

CHOOSING A HEALTHY BIRD

Now that you have made the decision to buy an Amazon parrot for a pet, you must be able to choose a healthy specimen. Once in the pet shop, step back and observe all of the birds offered for sale. If they are housed in separate cages, spend some time observing each bird. If housed collectively, pick out one bird at a time and carefully watch its interaction with the others. A healthy Amazon will climb around on the bars of the cage effortlessly. It will hang from one foot or the other and sometimes from a single toe. The healthy bird has an active interest in its surroundings and should be engaged in some activity other than sleeping. It may be at the feed dish, playing by itself or preening another bird's feathers. Some birds enjoy shadow boxing with an unseen adversary.

When you spot the active birds, pick out one that interests you and make a careful examination of the bird's overall condition. Is the plumage smooth and even, or ragged? Under no circumstances should any bare skin be visible through the feathers. Are the eyes clear and bright? Discharges from the eyes or swelling and scales on the eye rings indicate illness. The Amazon should look you right in the eye and not avoid your stare.

The eye rings of the Amazon should be clean and free from swelling.

The nasal openings must be free of dirt or discharge, have a round not irregular shape, and be free of sores or scales. The beak should have no discolorations, and the upper mandible must fit properly over the lower. The edges of the beak should be smooth and have no apparent worn surfaces. Look carefully at the bird's breast. Is the respiration slow and even or irregular? Avoid parrots with rapid, shallow or labored respiration. If the parrot of your choice meets the preceding criteria, have the pet shop employee remove it from the cage and examine it further. Look at the feet and toes. Are they free of sores? Are the pads worn? Is the parrot missing any toes? A missing toe or claw is not a severe handicap to the bird as long as there is no evidence of recent injury. Are the claws badly overgrown? Are the scales of the feet and legs smooth and even or raised and discolored? Place your finger in the grip of one foot at a time; is the grip even? Is one foot much hotter than the other or are

Above: *Alert eyes are one of the best indicators of a good candidate for taming.*
Opposite: *A beautiful Amazon pictured in natural surroundings.*

the feet unusually cold? Feel the parrot's breast. Is the breastbone protruding? A healthy bird has plenty of meat on either side of the breastbone and is said to have good weight. Baby birds should have good weight just as older birds. If you think that the bird is thin, do not purchase it even though it passes the other tests for good health. Thin birds often harbor some sort of malady and should not be purchased. The vent must be clean and have no evidence of soiling. Examine the wings, especially the clipped wing. There should be no lumps or sore spots at the base of the feathers.

You should also look carefully at the droppings in the cage. Healthy parrots have droppings of solid form. There should be both dark green and white matter in the droppings. Feces that are red-brown, orange, yellow, lime green, all white or very watery indicate that the birds have some physical disorder. Never purchase a parrot with offcolor or watery droppings.

When you ask the pet shop employee to hold the bird for you to examine, he should be willing to cooperate. Experienced bird handlers will not back away from this important task. The prospective buyer should not buy parrots from those who do not know how to handle them.

To review, the healthy Amazon parrot is an active bird, not one that sits ruffled up trying to sleep, ignoring its environment. It will have an alert expression and clear, bright eyes. Plumage will be smooth and even, not chewed. Nostrils will be clean and free, regularly shaped. Respiration will be slow and even, originating from the breast, not the throat. Feet and legs will have no wounds or raised scales. Claws will be a proper length. The mandibles will fit together properly and have no excessive wearing. The vent will be clean. Droppings will be dark green and white, of solid form. The parrot will have good weight. The breastbone will not protrude. The base of feathers on the wings and tail will not have any sores, lumps or bumps. The feet will have even heat and not be cold to the touch. Both feet will have equal gripping strength.

THE BEST CANDIDATE FOR TAMING

The best candidate for taming is a healthy bird that is eating well. Young parrots are the easiest to tame. An Amazon under one year of age is a rare find. A two- to three-year-old is still very young.

Opposite: *A beautiful pair of Amazon parrots. Under no circumstances should you purchase a bird that seems to be underweight.*

Five- to ten-year-old Amazons can be successfully tamed but often require more time to become really affectionate pets.

The parrot's personality is the most important factor for the trainer to observe. Steady birds that make eye contact with you are a good choice. If a parrot actively avoids looking into your eyes, think twice before buying it. An Amazon that listens to your voice is showing its desire for attention. Birds that rear up and try to frighten you with their display of aggression are often more easily tamed than shy birds that run from your approach. Timid birds can be tamed with time and patience, but many respond very slowly to your honest attempts to make friends. Frantic birds that smash themselves against the cage wire without regard for their personal safety are extremely difficult to tame.

When a parrot shows interest in your attention and moves over to the side of its cage to be closer to you, cocks its head to listen to your voice or verbalizes at you, it is indicating its tamability. By all means purchase this Amazon and take it home.

Transporting the bird from the pet shop to the home should be done with care. Many shops provide small cardboard carriers with ventilation holes. These are ideal. They protect the bird from drafts and changes in temperature, and they restrict its view of strange cars and people. Parrots often experience stress when confronted with unfamiliar noises and environments.

The new parrot should not be transported in the rain or snow. Have the shop keep it in a separate cage for you until the weather clears. You will probably be purchasing a cage from them anyway. If possible, bring the bird home early in the day to give it plenty of time to adjust to the new surroundings before bedtime. The first day with your new parrot is often the ideal time to begin taming. Many people feel it is necessary to give the bird one or two weeks to settle down before beginning the taming process. With some nervous birds this may be advisable, but the majority respond well to taming if it is started immediately.

The parrot should not be placed in a cage with another parrot (perhaps another family pet) while you are taming it. Some people think that a single bird will be lonely. If you spend time with the parrot it will not be lonely and will look to you for attention. Desire for attention is the main reason that parrots are so trainable!

Two Amazons that live compatibly together often develop aggressive attitudes towards any interference from people or other birds. Pairs of birds are best left alone. Attempting to tame one member of the pair or both is often futile. Although you may be able to

Before purchasing your Amazon parrot, it is a good idea to assemble the necessary equipment and to find a permanent place for the cage.

hand train them, you will probably never get any further in developing a good pet/owner relationship.

WHAT YOU WILL NEED TO BEGIN

You should obtain the necessary equipment before bringing the parrot home from the shop. Many people buy the bird first and worry about the accessories later. This usually

leads to poor feeding during the first few days when it is imperative to get the bird off to a good start. An adequate cage must be provided from the first day, not when the budget can afford it. Taming the bird cannot wait for some future date when the proper equipment is secured.

The parrot cage must be made of metal, not wood or plastic. It must have enough room for the bird to stand in the middle and flap its wings without touching the sides. Minimum dimensions for most Amazon varieties are 20 inches square, 24 inches high. Some larger birds such as the mealy or blue-crowned may require larger cages. Nickel-plated cages hold up very well and are easily maintained. Brassplated cages tend to discolor more readily than nickel. Painted metal is not recommended. Paint chips and is hard to keep in tip-top shape. If you have a painted metal cage and plan to recondition it for a new bird, be certain to clean it completely and use paint that is non-toxic when dry. The words "non-toxic when dry" must appear on the label, or don't use the paint. Parrot cages are constructed of standard heavy parrot wire with the wire spaced about one inch apart to accommodate the parrot in climbing around. All parrot cages should have a removable grill above the bottom tray to keep the bird out of the feces and food that fall through. The door must be large enough for the parrot to move through without touching the sides when sitting on your hand. Small doors make the task of moving the bird in and out difficult. The cage can be either plain or ornamented, as long as the parrot has adequate room to climb around and exercise.

Perches made of natural wood provide many different grips for the Amazon's feet. This helps to keep the feet healthy and the claws in good shape. Dowel perches must be one inch in diameter. Smaller diameters will cause cramps in the bird's feet. Most parrot cages have one perch in the center of the cage. If you have a larger cage you may want to place additional perches in it. This is fine as long as you don't clutter up the bird's living space. There is no need for sandpaper fittings on the perches.

Give the Amazon a swing or a sturdy ring to play on. The bird will play more with a swing than you would imagine.

Bird stands serve many needs for both parrot and owner. A stand is recommended for taming the parrot since hand taming a parrot while it sits in its cage is more difficult and time consuming. Stands give the parrot freedom in the house without giving it the run of the house. You can easily move the stand from room to room and even out in the yard.

Many retail bird shops offer a variety of bird stands for sale. Hanging stands are fine for tame birds, but are not very good for taming the bird. Table stands lack the stability of the floor models. The floor stand may come with a cage cover that fits over the perch and sits on a tray. These are popular because it makes it easy to get the bird out into the open without having to get it through a door. A stand separate from the cage is recommended. The simple T-style is best for taming. If you decide to make your own stand, be certain to provide a sturdy base.

Feed and water cups must be made of material that is easy to clean. Most parrot cages come with two hard plastic cups. If they become broken or discolored after many years of use, your pet shop usually sells replacement cups of the same type. Glass or ceramic feeders are fine. Metal cups are good for seed, but not as good for water. Clay cups should not be used. The size of the feeders depends upon the number of birds in the cage. Obviously community cages require bigger, more sturdy feeders and waterers than single cages. Placement on the cage bottom is not recommended, for the feed and water may become soiled with feces.

Bird toys are sold in specialty shops or can be made at home. Don't clutter up the cage with toys.

Different birds will have different reactions to people approaching their cage. Some will retreat to the back of the cage, some will stare right back, and others will put on a show of aggression.

A white-fronted Amazon parrot. When shopping for your Amazon, try to choose a bird that is less than three years old.

Put one toy in the cage and use others on the training stand or keep them aside to play with the bird yourself. Good parrot toys are ladders, bells with secure clappers, heavy chains and sturdy metal rings, and nylon dog bones to name a few. Mirrors attract the bird to its own image and should not be placed in the cage. The goal is for the bird to be interested in you, not its own reflection. Mirrors can also interfere with speech training. Parrot playgrounds can be purchased at retail bird shops. These are fine, but don't let the parrot play there for hours on end. You must structure the parrot's time outside of the cage for taming and training to progress satisfactorily. Toys are not considered priority items when you first buy the bird.

For taming it is useful to have two short dowels, 18 to 24 inches long, and one long dowel, three feet long. All training sticks should be one inch in diameter.

Bird nets come in handy in the aviary setting when you have to catch a bird that flies. Nets should not be used in the taming lesson, but may be useful if your parrot climbs into an inaccessible place. Do not use the net to retrieve the parrot routinely or you will never make a friend out of it. For emergencies, you can capture a parrot with a towel; the method will be described later.

The novice bird tamer may want to buy gloves to use in the taming sessions. These are not recommended, but if you are determined to use gloves, buy the tight fitting leather golf gloves that are available at sport shops. Gloves should be beige or some other neutral shade. Colorful or bulky gloves scare the parrot, making taming more difficult.

Have the proper feed available for the bird from the first day. Buy sunflower seed from your pet shop or farm supply. Sunflower seed from the market is less expensive, but it also is less nourishing.

Wooden dowels are essential pieces of equipment for stick-training. At least two dowels are necessary for this process.

Some pet shops offer special parrot mix, with peanuts, peppers and dried corn. Buy raw corn on the cob, bananas, apples and oranges at the market and feed these on a daily basis. A variety of fruits and vegetables can be given. Have some raw peanuts to add to the seed, unless you are using parrot mix.

You should provide a gravel mixture periodically although it is not necessary to have it in the cage at all times. A mineral block or cuttlebone should be present at all times in the cage. Supplements to the diet should be given daily. Water soluble vitamins are manufactured specially for birds and can be bought at the bird shop. A powdered supplement adds important minerals to the diet when sprinkled on the bird's fruit and vegetables. Cod liver or wheat germ oil should be used sparingly on the seed to keep plumage in good shape.

Feeding, Cleaning, and General Care

Sunflower seed or parrot mix should be changed daily. Most people feed and water their pets in the morning before they leave for work. Give the bird a small slice of apple, orange, or other fruit along with a piece of raw corn. Other fruits that can be given are melon, pear, peach, banana, or whatever is fresh and available. Always let fruit and vegetables warm to room temperature before giving them to the parrot. Vegetables that your Amazon may enjoy are squash, boiled potato, peas, beans, carrots and celery to name a few. There is no need to overload your bird with soft foods. A good formula is one green and one yellow vegetable, one fruit and a slice of citrus daily. These will balance the diet.

Smaller seeds including oats, hemp, and safflower can be given to parrots. Some even enjoy white millet or the spray millet that is marketed for smaller birds.

Put a squirt of oil on the seed every other day. This is not to suggest that any form of oil or fat is good for your Amazon. Use only the recommended oils: wheat germ or cod liver.

Every morning when you change the bird's water, scrub the cup with hot water and soap. Cleaning the water cup daily is one of the best ways of protecting your Amazon against illness. Some people use well water for their pet parrots. Well water is high in mineral content. By using the recommended vitamin and mineral supplements you will provide a well-balanced diet for your Amazon, so don't overdo it.

Treats for the Amazon include low-calorie millet sprays, fresh branches from trees complete with leaves (just use a small cutting), and monkey chow biscuits or dog biscuits. Stay away from ice cream, chocolate and cake. Many parrots enjoy sweet-tasting foods, but overweight is one of the most common health hazards for household pets. In later life parrots can suffer from obesity that may lead to heart disease. When giving fresh branches, be certain that your cuttings are free from insecticides and the feces of other birds. Branches from elm, oak, maple and fruit trees, as well as from some bushes like hibiscus or cherry hedge, are fine for the Amazon.

Cleaning the bird and his cage should be done routinely. Give the Amazon a sturdy dish of warm water to bathe in. Some parrots enjoy being misted, and this is a good opportunity for you to play with the bird. Others dislike

Opposite: *A nutritious diet will go a long way towards keeping your Amazon parrot happy and healthy throughout its life.*

misting and become upset at the sight of the spray bottle. Use your common sense and don't spray the bird if it objects. Chances are that once your relationship has progressed, the bird may change its mind about misting. Use plain warm water for bathing the Amazon. Feather-shine sprays can be used safely, but the plumage will have natural sheen if the diet is right.

Never bathe the bird at night or on cold, stormy days. Give the bath early in the day to allow the feathers to dry thoroughly before sundown. In the summer it is safe to bathe the Amazon every day, but this is not necessary. One or two baths a week are plenty. Don't bathe the newly arrived Amazon until it has been eating well for at least a week and has had time to adjust to new surroundings. After the first bath you'll be surprised at how much better the bird will look. Parrots don't like to be dirty, and in the wild or in outdoor aviaries they bathe in the rain, spreading out their wings to catch every drop.

You should spray your bird's cage periodically with commercially made bird bug

A lovely pair of Amazon parrots. Amazons are naturally clean birds, and most will enjoy an occasional bath.

An Amazon parrot gnawing on a toy ring. Pet shops offer a variety of cage toys which will entertain the Amazon for hours. Be careful, however, not to overcrowd the cage with them.

spray. Your pet shop will carry one or two different kinds. Household pets usually do not suffer from bug infestation, so spraying the cage is often good enough. You may want to spray the new bird after it has had time to settle in. New birds may bring in bugs from their previous residence. Parrots that live outdoors should have the aviary cage sprayed at least once a month. If there is evidence of parasite infestation on the birds, it

may be necessary to catch each parrot and treat it individually. One spraying should do the trick if the cage is treated more often.

Clean the cage bottom often. Daily cleaning is best. Newspaper on the cage bottom is fine if changed daily and if the Amazon does not chew it up. Some Amazons attack the newspaper as soon as it is placed into the cage and chew it to shreds; for these birds use wood shavings on the cage bottom. Shavings can be spot-cleaned daily and changed every few days. Sand on the cage bottom is fine in the outdoor cage, but is not recommended, since it does not provide a soft cushion on the cage bottom if the parrot should fall to the ground. Sand also may harbor internal and external bird parasites.

Clean the bottom grill and cage bars with plain water. You may have to clean the grill with a stiff brush to remove food and fecal residues. Dry the cage bars thoroughly after washing to prevent rust. Cleaning the cage regularly will keep it shining and in good shape for years. The bottom tray should be washed often and must be cleaned with hot water and mild detergent to disinfect it.

Perches and swings should be cleaned with a perch scraper or sandpaper to remove dirt and keep the surface from becoming too hard. Hard perches will wear down the pads on the bird's feet. If you must wash the perches, let them dry completely before replacing them in the cage. If an Amazon stands on wet or damp perches it can develop a variety of illnesses.

Wash and dry feed dishes at least once a week, more often if required.

Cover the cage at night if it is very cold or damp. In the summer it is not necessary to cover the cage unless it is raining or windy. Cage covers should be made of lightweight material. Frayed edges are dangerous to your parrot. Sew them down or use another cover and wash the cover periodically. If you are going to have a party, either move the cage to another room or cover the parrot at a reasonable hour.

Manicure the parrot's claws as needed. Overgrown claws can cause foot problems. At the proper length, claws rest comfortably on the perch or your arm, giving the bird a secure grip with toes extended. When the claws scratch you it is time for a manicure.

CLIPPING THE WING AND CLAWS

Clipping the wing of the Amazon to facilitate taming is recommended. Only clip one wing. By clipping both, you give the parrot too much direction over its flight, but with one wing clipped the bird is unable to fly in a

Opposite: *The claws of the Amazon parrot will sometimes overgrow and need clipping. Before undertaking this procedure, learn the proper method from an experienced professional.*

straight line. Learn to clip the wing of your new parrot by first having an experienced person show you how.

First you must know how to capture and hold the parrot. Take the bird out of its cage and, if possible, slip your hand over its head, grasping it with your thumb beneath the lower mandible with the rest of your fingers cradling the head and neck. Use a towel to cover your lap. With your other hand hold the bird's torso, one or two fingers between the legs. With a wild bird, you may have to use a net or towel. After netting the parrot, have someone assist you in removing it from the net. First get the legs, then the head. Place your thumb beneath the lower mandible. When using a towel to capture a parrot, place the bird on the floor. Drop the towel over its head and grab it around the head and neck from behind. Hold the torso, with one or two fingers between the legs, against your towel-covered lap.

Be careful not to twist the neck or legs. Hold the bird gently and don't restrict its breathing. Don't pull or push on the neck. The holder is responsible for watching the bird's respiration and eyes and must be calm enough to hold the bird still without hurting it.

Gather all of the necessary supplies before beginning to clip the wing. A sharp pair of scissors, a small wire clipper, and ample light are all you will need.

With the holder doing his job, extend the wings and look at both. Leave the better feathered wing alone. Hold the wing to be clipped firmly at the bend of the wing. Leave the two outer feathers as they are and clip the next two in half. Now take the wire clippers and clip off the next seven or eight feathers at the point where the feather begins to emerge from the shaft. Always be certain to leave at least one inch of feather shaft emerging from the edge of the wing.

You must be able to identify blood feathers from growing feathers before attempting to clip the wing. Blood feathers are new feathers that have not finished growing in. All new feathers from the smallest to the largest begin as blood feathers. All of these new feathers are nourished by a vein that is connected to the internal vascular system. When the feather has grown in, the vein dries up and seals off at the feather follicle. If a blood feather is cut by accident, the bird will bleed until the blood clots or the feather is pulled. For this reason it is important that the person clipping is experienced in this procedure.

Clipping the claws can be done at the same time you clip the wing. Always have a styptic powder on hand to stop bleeding if a claw is cut too short. Be careful not to cut too much off the claw or it will bleed. When bleeding occurs, use the styptic powder to help the

Amazon parrots preen themselves frequently. Sometimes a breeding pair will help preen each other.

blood clot. Pack a small amount of the powder against the bleeding tip and press. Bleeding usually stops in a few moments. Styptic powder is better than a styptic pencil; the pencil is too hard.

After clipping all eight claws, use a nail file to smooth off the edge of each one. Some Amazons become tame enough for their owners to file their claws while they sit on their stand.

When the claws are badly overgrown it is best to just clip off a bit at a time to avoid hitting blood. It may take a couple of weeks before the claws are down to a normal length.

Taming the Amazon Parrot

The trainer can be either a man or a woman. In the initial taming sessions only one person should work with the bird. Two people tend to distract one another and make the bird nervous. The best trainer is the person with the most time to devote to the task. The trainer must not be a quitter and should have a calm, cool head. Some Amazons take much longer to tame than others, and if the trainer is impatient or inconsistent in his lessons, the parrot may never develop the desired behavior. Nervous people are poor choices for trainers, as are people with quick tempers who may end up injuring the bird. The person with self-confidence who knows that he can accomplish taming the parrot given enough time is the best possible choice. Young children should not be responsible for taming the Amazon. Besides the possibility of being bitten by the bird, the average child cannot understand the reason that the parrot is biting. Lacking proper understanding of the parrot, they may harm it or develop bad feelings toward it.

The taming area should be decided upon before you begin. A small room is better than a large one. A carpeted or padded floor is imperative to protect the bird from injury. Rooms with a great deal of furniture are difficult to work in, for the bird may be difficult to retrieve. A cluttered room is hazardous to the parrot if it insists on jumping away from you or the bird stand.

Cover large windows and mirrors that the parrot may be attracted to. If the room has no carpeting, be certain to pad the floor. Bring the cage into the training area in the first couple of lessons until you have taught the parrot to remain on a stick while you move him from room to room.

Have a low birdstand available and two training sticks, one short, one long. Bring a few food rewards and the bird's water cup into the training area. Tie back your hair to keep it out of the way and remove bracelets and rings that may attract the parrot. Wear a shirt that the bird cannot get its claws snagged in or you may be bitten unnecessarily.

THE FIRST LESSONS

Place the bird cage low to the floor and open the door. Step back and see if the bird will come out of the cage. If not, offer it a stick to perch on and try to move it through the door. It may help to stand behind the cage, for the parrot may walk away from you out the open door. Most birds will

Opposite: *Before the taming session begins, be sure the taming area is free from dangerous obstacles, harmful drafts, and other birds.*

Taming the Amazon Parrot

Stick-training is the first step in the taming process.

climb to the top of the cage once out. Slowly close the cage door without startling the bird.

You must learn to move slowly around parrots even after they are tame. By moving slowly and deliberately, the parrot will have a chance to observe you and see that you intend no harm. With the cage door closed, the parrot cannot jump back into the cage. Using the short training stick, place it in front of the parrot's feet. Push gently against the bird's legs in an upward motion. Some birds will run all over the cage rather than step on the stick, while others will step up as though they've been doing it for years. For those that run, try to maneuver them off of the cage onto the floor. Step

between the parrot and its cage and kneel down, offering the stick. Most parrots prefer to get off the floor. If necessary, slowly corner the bird and keep offering the stick until it steps on.

When the parrot steps onto the stick for the first time, do not lift it high off the floor. If the bird stepped onto the stick as soon as it was offered, move slowly to the stand and let it step on. With these steady Amazons, taming is often achieved in the first lesson. For birds that step onto the stick and jump off every couple of seconds, drill low to the floor. Let the bird step onto the stick and put it back down on the floor. Repeat this drill until the bird steps unhesitatingly onto the stick. At this point move the bird to the stand and let it step on.

Teach the parrot to step from the stand to the stick, and back again, by drilling it over and over. Speak to the Amazon in a soft, soothing voice as you drill it. Never grab the bird, and don't chase after it if it jumps off the stand to the floor. Always move slowly and the bird will settle down faster. Retrieve it with the stick and go back to the stand.

After you feel that the bird has mastered stick training, begin hand taming. Offer your hand to the parrot, not your finger. Most Amazons are too large to sit on your finger. Offer your hand, fingers together, horizontally to the bird's feet. Some parrots will lift one foot and hold it in the air.

Once the bird has mastered his stick-training lessons, hand taming may begin.

Others will step on with one foot and leave the other gripping the stand. Most parrots test new perches by pressing against them with their beaks. If the Amazon steps on with one foot and moves its beak down to touch your hand, don't assume that the bird will bite you. The natural tendency of a novice trainer is to draw away from the parrot's beak. This is very bad. It signifies to the parrot that you are not a reliable perch.

This is not to suggest that you let the parrot bite you. Most of the time the bird will not bite you anyway, but if you do have to deal with a parrot that bites, learn to use your free hand to distract it. Use one hand to push against the bird's feet, but don't push with one constant motion if it does not step onto your hand. Press against the legs for an instant and then relax the pressure without moving your hand away. Constant pressure may cause the Amazon to hold tightly to the stand. Intermittent pressure usually causes the bird to release its grip in order to balance.

You may have to coax the bird with a food reward. Try sunflower seed, peanuts, or raw corn kernels. Reward the bird for placing one foot on your hand and go from there. When he places one foot on your hand, press against the other leg and move your hand in a slow upward motion. The bird may step on immediately or the lesson could

take a long time. You must be able to adjust to the bird's behavior if you are going to be successful at taming. Don't let the parrot train you, but learn to shape the length and content of the lessons according to the parrot's responses.

If the bird bites you every time you offer your hand, tell it "NO" in a loud voice when it moves to bite. Use your free hand to distract the bird by touching it lightly if necessary. Never strike the parrot for biting you. Not only could you injure the bird, but you won't get the lesson across. Be patient, consistent, and even-tempered if you plan to tame the bird.

When the parrot steps onto your hand for the first time, slowly move your hand away from the stand. Let the bird remain on your hand for as long as you can. Talk to it in a low voice and give it as much food reward as it will take.

After placing the parrot back on the stand, offer your hand again immediately in the same manner as before. When the bird steps onto your hand the first few times, you have made a definite breakthrough. Practice having the bird step onto your hand from the stand and back again to make this an automatic response.

Repetition of basic behaviors is the best way to tame your parrot. Stick training and hand taming are the most basic forms of training that you can do with a parrot. After the parrot steps onto your hand fluidly, move your hand away from the stand and slowly turn your back to it. Use your body to block the bird from jumping back to the stand. Hold your hand and elbow low and in close to your body. Talk to the parrot. In a few minutes, turn back to the stand and let the bird step back on if it wants. Give it a drink of water and begin again.

Taming lessons do not have to be marathon sessions of an hour or more. Twenty minutes of intensive work is enough for parrot and trainer alike. Learn how to relax while the bird sits on its stand; the bird will need to rest and let the lesson sink in anyway. Let the parrot sit on the stand even if you leave the room for a minute. Teaching the bird to remain on the stand is one of your ultimate goals.

If you decide to leave the house or get involved in a lengthy chore, put the bird back in its cage and resume the lesson later.

After the parrot has mastered hand taming, try to walk slowly around the room with it. Talk to the bird. Stand still, then move some more. Eventually leave the taming area and walk slowly to another room. Hold your hand down and give the bird the security of your body. Holding the parrot up in the air and walking with it will invite the bird to jump. When you get to the other room, stand still for a minute and talk to the bird. Then walk some more. This is the best way of

After about fifteen minutes of training, give the bird a rest. Short, frequent lessons are recommended more than long, intensive sessions.

familiarizing the bird with your home and getting it to accept you as the most secure perch available. At this point, you should be able to continue your lessons in the same room the cage is in. Move the stand into the room and continue the lessons.

When the parrot is relaxed enough to perch on your hand, introduce it to the other family members. One at a time should attempt to make friends with the bird. When one person deals with a parrot exclusively, it often develops into a one-man or one-woman bird. The one-person bird is not desirable in a family setting. Amazons can be very jealous of people that live in the house who don't pay attention to them. Avoid the one-person bird by proper training. If you can't solve the problem, at least keep others away from the parrot or it may inflict a painful bite.

Frequent lessons are important in taming and training a parrot to coexist in a household. Deal with the Amazon on a daily basis, more than once a day if possible. Once the bird has mastered the basics, take it out of the cage and let it sit on the stand in the family room as much as possible. Place the bird back in its cage when you are ready to retire for the night.

There are some myths about parrot taming that should be discussed. Taming the bird in a totally dark room is foolish. The bird can't see and neither can you. Both parties will get nervous under these circumstances. Have adequate lighting in the training area. Wetting the bird is a bad idea since it subjects the bird to additional stress in an already stressful situation. Never wet the bird for reasons of training. Food deprivation is thought by some to be a good way of winning the bird's confidence. On the contrary! A hungry bird is more interested in eating than in making friends with you. Part of winning the bird's

confidence is accomplished by feeding and watering it regularly. You may wish to cut the ration of feed during training into two or more portions, giving one portion in the morning and the rest in the afternoon and evening.

Chaining the parrot to the stand is inhumane and dangerous. Some parrots will learn to live with the leg chain, but the majority react to it by trying to chew it off or pull the foot free. The bird that is suddenly frightened may jump off the stand and break its leg if held by a chain. It is far better to put the time into perch training if you wish the parrot to remain out for any length of time. Teach the parrot to remain on the stand by letting it sit there and then reward it periodically for sitting. Pick it up on your hand, place it back on the stand, and reward it.

Petting the bird takes additional training. Touch the parrot on the breast for an instant and talk to it. You may have to put a good deal of time into pet taming before the bird actually enjoys being touched. Most Amazons learn to love having their heads scratched. Eventually the parrot will hold up all of the feathers on the head and neck for you to preen. In the initial lessons, try stroking the bird on the beak, throat, nape, and face. Rub his toes and legs. Try touching it under the wings. Find out what your parrot accepts the easiest and go from there. You must learn to adjust your training

Once the bird is hand tame, the owner can carry the bird from room to room.

to the responses of the bird; not all parrots enjoy the same kind of handling.

Developing a friendly rapport with an Amazon may take from a few days to a few months. Don't be discouraged if the bird does not adjust quickly. Give yourself and the parrot plenty of time and sincere effort before giving up trying to tame it.

It is possible that you may encounter an untamable Amazon parrot. Most of the time these are older parrots that have lived for many years in someone's home. The former owners probably never handled the bird, so it adjusted to a life of confinement without much human interaction. It is unlikely that you will ever be able to make this a pettable bird. Parrots that have lived for years with people that did handle them are often slow to make friends with new owners, but it is possible.

The great majority of imported birds are very tamable if they come to you from the wholesaler or retailer. These parrots have had no previous experience as household pets, so they have not developed any rigid ideas of how to behave with people. If you give the wild bird an opportunity to develop positive attitudes toward life as a single pet, you will most likely end up with an affectionate bird. It is far easier to tame a wild-caught Amazon than one that has been ignored in someone's home for many years.

You can consider your Amazon a tame pet if it exhibits the following behavior. It will come out of the cage when you open the door even if it comes out by itself for a couple of weeks. Once outside the cage the bird will step onto your hand from the cage to be transferred to the stand. The parrot will remain sitting on the stand for a period of time without jumping off. The bird will step onto your hand from the stand and remain there without biting. The bird will step from one hand to the other. At this point you can allow other family members to begin handling the bird. Always supervise children or you may have to deal with an injured parrot or child. Let the adult members of the household make friends with the parrot. Try not to stand and watch their first interactions or you will make both parties nervous. Remember that it is very important

for the Amazon to become tame to more than one person or you will end up with a one-man or one-woman bird. Avoid this situation by having more than one person feed, clean and handle the parrot.

SPECIAL BEHAVIOR PROBLEMS

Biting is one of the most common behavior problems that pet owners report. It is important to understand why the bird is biting. Is the bird fear-biting or biting out of aggression? Fear-biting can usually be cured if you devote enough time to the task. Spend time feeding the bird out of your hand. If it refuses to eat from your hand or reaches past the food and bites you, change the feeding time from morning to afternoon. Feed the bird out of your hand before placing the feed dish back in the cage. Don't skip the bird's meal completely. If the bird is really stubborn, give it a half ration of feed and sit right next to the bird as it eats.

If you persist with this program, the parrot will soon learn to eat from your hand. Never skip the feeding for a whole day. If you don't have time for the lesson, feed the bird anyway, but do it in the afternoon. Stick to the schedule. Fear biting will abate when the bird loses its fear of you. This may take awhile.

Aggressive biting is more difficult to deal with. Most parrots will not bite unless provoked, but some will bite as soon as you are in range. With these parrots, you should use some hand and arm protection. Don't wear bulky gloves or jackets. Tight-fitting garments afford much more protection, for the bird cannot get a firm hold. Tuck your fingers under your hand when trying to get the bird to step on. Again, change the feeding time to afternoon or evening, after training is finished for the night. Try feeding the bird out of your hand. If it tries to bite you, say a loud "NO" and use your free hand to distract it. You must learn to be

quick enough to read your bird's behavior, for most give a twenty-second warning before biting you. Pay attention to what you are doing and you won't be bitten too often.

Do a great deal of drill with the training stick and tire the bird out before attempting to get it on your hand. If it tries to bite again, go back to the stick. This is the time for the marathon taming session. Don't make the bird frantic but be determined and cool-headed. Just keep drilling the bird until it finally gives in. It may take an hour or longer. Use your common sense;

After the initial trainer has completed hand taming, other people may begin to work with the bird.

let the bird rest if it pants uncontrollably, but the point of the session is to break the bird of a very bad habit. Don't let it sit for five minutes until it begins to respond to the lesson. One or two intensive lessons like this can often cure an aggressive bird from biting you, but keep in mind that this bird would probably vent his anger on another person. Acclimate this bird to the other family members more carefully.

Do not hit a parrot for biting you. This will not cure the problem and may make it even worse. If you can't deal with the bird at all, try to find a more experienced person to help you.

Clipping the beak to make the bite less severe is a very bad idea, and should never be done. This does not make the bite softer and can cause a great deal of harm to the bird. Beaks should be clipped only if overgrown.

Amazon parrots that scream for attention can be very annoying. Remember that the parrots are noisy birds in the morning and afternoon. It is natural for most birds to herald the sunrise and sunset, so if you can't live with some noise, don't buy a parrot. Cure a bird that screams for attention by structuring your day to spend more time with the bird. Most people make the mistake of paying attention to the parrot when it is screaming. This is just what the bird has in mind, since screaming obviously gets the desired result. Try to ignore the bird when it screams. Cover the cage for a few minutes and uncover it as soon as it has been quiet for three or four minutes. The time to pay attention to the bird is when you uncover it. Talk to it and take it out of the cage. Reward the bird for the correct behavior, in this case, for not screaming. Be consistent and the screaming should become less of a problem.

Birds that destroy your possessions need more supervision. Parrots are chewers and there is no way to change that. Some are more avid chewers than others. Give your parrot plenty of wood to chew to direct its energy. Fresh branches or 3-inch to 4-inch lengths of 1 x 1 inch lumber should be given daily.

Feather chewing is not a common problem with Amazon parrots. Birds that chew their feathers are usually not eating a balanced diet, suffering from parasite infestation or exhibiting anxiety. Check the diet and correct it if necessary. Make sure that the supplements to the diet are being given regularly. If the diet is correct, examine the bird for parasites. These are hard to detect with the naked eye, but if the bird has dropped a large feather, examine it under a good light to see if there are any tiny spots moving near the quill. It may be wise to treat the bird and its cage for parasites even if you

The Amazon parrot and its owner will learn quite a lot from each other during the taming process.

can't see any. If you think that the bird is nervous or displaying anxiety, try to distract it by providing more chewing material. Spend more time with the bird when you are home. Give it as much time out of the cage as possible. Feather chewing may persist until the clipped wing has grown out or the bird is bought a companion. Try to decide what is best for the bird. If you don't have enough time for the parrot, give it to someone who does.

Training For Speech and Tricks

SPEECH TRAINING

Amazon parrots are excellent mimics. Given regular lessons, they can become fluent talkers. The most reliable of the Amazons for speech are the yellow-naped, Mexican double yellow-head, yellow-fronted, yellow-crowned, blue-crowned and blue-fronted. These are just a few of the better birds for speech.

There is considerable variation from bird to bird within any given species. Parrots like the orange-winged or lilac-crowned may not have the reputation for being great talkers, but many of them are.

No matter what type of Amazon you buy, you can expect at least one or two words. The amount and quality of the parrot's speech depends most upon the trainer. People that make the effort to teach the bird are usually rewarded for their work. It is best to have a single pet for speech training. Keep mirrors away from the bird. Give lessons at least once or twice a day. Try to use the bird's natural desire to vocalize in the morning and afternoon by giving your lessons at those times. Only one person should teach the bird to speak its first words.

Have the bird sit on its stand or in its cage and teach it one word at a time. Begin with "Hello" followed by the bird's name. A one- or two-syllable name is easiest for the bird to learn. Repeat the word "Hello" distinctly and slowly every few seconds.

Have food rewards on hand to give the parrot as soon as it makes any sound in response to your "Hello." Don't expect to have the bird duplicate your speech at first. In the first lessons, reward the parrot for any vocalization at the appropriate time. Work closer and closer to the word as the lessons progress. Once the bird vocalizes for you consistently, listen for a two-syllable sound and reward immediately. The parrot will soon attach the reward with its imitation. Some birds attain the first word quickly, while others take eight weeks or more. Once the first word is repeated by the parrot consistently, you can begin to teach a second word.

The second and third words should be simple. Limit the number of syllables that you expect the bird to duplicate. After "Hello," a two-syllable sound, go to "How are you?" or "Hi sweetie," which are both three-syllable sounds. Build your parrot's vocabulary as you would a child's. At first, teach simple words and phrases; later go on to phrases with many syllables.

Opposite: *Amazon parrots are intelligent birds that are capable of learning a number of tricks.*

Training For Speech and Tricks

Parrots can learn short musical phrases also. Whatever you decide to teach, stick with it until the bird says it. If you try to teach two different things at once, the bird will have a hard time learning either.

Tape-recorded speech lessons work, but are not recommended. The goal is for the parrot to talk to you, not a tape recorder. Most people put on the recording when they go to work or out for the evening. The parrot may learn to speak, but not with people present. The fact is, it may speak very well when no one is there but say nothing with people around. If you want to use tapes to supplement your live lessons, go ahead, but make certain to still give the live lesson every day.

You can teach your bird to speak without standing in front of it, but the bird probably won't talk on command. Command speech means that the bird will repeat after you whenever you want it to. Even if you don't have time for command speech training, you should talk to your parrot as you get ready for work in the morning, while you service its cage, or do household chores. A parrot that talks is lots of fun, and a happier bird. Even if it doesn't talk on command, you'll be amazed at how well parrots can imitate the human voice.

It is not necessary to darken the room or cover the cage for speech lessons. Don't try to teach the parrot to speak with television or music in the background. Work in a quiet room and pay all of your attention to the lesson. An old wives' tale still persists that splitting the bird's tongue will facilitate speech. This is a cruel idea and should never be done. Such treatment can kill the bird and does absolutely nothing to improve its speech. Parrots speak well because of their excellent hearing and the physiology of their tongue, throat and vocal cords.

There are two types of speech training worth discussing here. Imitative speech refers to the parrot repeating a phrase after it is said by the trainer; it is imitating the trainer's words. Responsive speech refers to the parrot replying to the trainer's phrase with an answer; it is responding to the trainer's words. For example, the parrot is imitating when the trainer says "Hi sweetie," and the bird answers "Hi sweetie." The parrot is responding when the trainer asks "What's your name?" and the bird replies "Sinbad."

To teach responsive speech, first teach the parrot the answer to your question or the reply to your statement. Work on the response until the parrot says it consistently. Then begin asking the question and reward the parrot for the appropriate response. It is important that the Amazon take food rewards in order to teach it responsive speech. This process is more difficult and time

Several species of Amazon parrot are considered to be good talkers. Teaching a parrot to talk requires the same patience and diligence as taming and training.

consuming than imitation, but well worth it.

People think it is impossible to teach older birds to talk. Truly, it is easier to teach a young bird, but some older parrots will learn to talk even though their speech may be limited to a few words. With young parrots it is possible to teach an unlimited amount of words, phrases and sounds. Remember to work on one thing at a time and build your parrot's repertoire slowly. Over eight or nine years an Amazon can develop an amazing vocabulary.

As long as you keep up the lessons consistently, the parrot will learn new words. After a while it becomes difficult to think of new things to teach the bird, but at this point you will have a really accomplished talking parrot.

ADVANCED TRAINING FOR TRICKS

As with speech, there is a great deal of variation in the ability of Amazons to perform tricks. Most are clever, and with regular lessons can learn to do a number of different things. Base the tricks

A well-trained Amazon parrot "playing dead." This is only one of the many tricks an Amazon is capable of learning.

Although two Amazons may be the best of friends, it is a good idea to train them separately until one has gained some experience in bird training.

to be taught on the bird's natural behaviors. Of course, the parrot must be tame and eating well. Work on only one trick at a time and reward for each repetition of the correct behavior. You will be more successful at trick training if you can touch the parrot.

Give short lessons many times during the day for the best results. If you give lessons for a week, skip a few days and then go back to training, don't expect the bird to learn anything. This type of irregularity can confuse a bird and ruin any chances of future trick

Patience is necessary for success in training your Amazon. **Left:** Starting under the bird's neck, run your hand slowly and gently down the chest to the feet; push gently but firmly against its feet so the bird will step onto your hand. **Below:** If this procedure doesn't work the first time, let the bird calm down and try again.

Right: When the bird steps onto your hand, give it a food reward. Trust is not always established between the bird and trainer immediately.
Below: Speak in a gentle voice and allow the bird to return to the perch. Resume training again when the bird is composed.

training. It is imperative that the parrot be able to master the tricks or it will learn to be unsuccessful. This is the worst orientation that you can give the parrot. Either follow through on your trick training or don't begin at all.

Amazons can learn to wave "Hello" by teaching them to move a foot when you say the word. The slightest movement should be rewarded in the initial lessons. As with speech, demand more as training progresses. Teach the bird to lie on its back in your hand. Turn it over for an instant and reward. Don't hold the parrot down for more than an instant. As it gets used to this handling, you can extend the period of time you keep it on its back. Always reward the bird for lying down.

Teach the Amazon to put coins or tokens in a piggy bank. First teach the bird to pick up the objects, then teach it to drop them in the coin slot. Hang a cup from the bird stand and place a peanut in it. Encourage the bird to pull the cup up for the peanut. This is a very simple trick for most Amazons.

Break down complex tasks into separate behaviors and teach in sequence. Don't teach complicated tricks first, but begin with simple tasks and work up to more difficult ones. Observe your parrot's normal behavior and think up your own tricks to teach the bird.

THINGS TO REMEMBER ABOUT TAMING AND TRAINING

Work with the Amazon parrot regularly, every day. Move slowly and deliberately around the bird. Speak to your parrot in a soft, soothing voice and use its name often. Work alone to avoid commotion. Many short lessons are more effective than a single long lesson. Do not use food deprivation in taming or training, but change the feeding time instead. Never strike the parrot.

Assemble all of the necessary equipment for taming the parrot and work in a prepared area. Be consistent in your approach to taming and training. Give the Amazon time to accept one trainer before having others handle the bird. Never leave the job of taming an Amazon to a child.

Be realistic in advanced training. Work from the simple to the difficult. Always reward your bird for the correct response, and work closer and closer to the desired goal.

Opposite: *Amazons love to climb and swing on chains. Take care, however, to provide chains that are safe; the wrong size chain can be hazardous to your pet.*

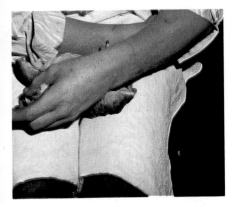

Left: *Sit and hold your bird securely in your lap when examination is necessary.* **Below:** *Cooperation during an examination should be no problem with a tame and responsive bird.*

Illness and First Aid

When you go to the store to buy accessories for the parrot, it is wise to invest in a few first aid preparations to have on hand in case of accidents. Buy styptic powder from your pet shop to stop bleeding from claws and feathers. Don't use it on skin wounds, as it burns. For skin wounds use hydrogen peroxide to disinfect and stop bleeding. Buy antiseptic powder at the pharmacy to dress wounds. Ask your pet shop for a good bird salve to use on sore feet or skin. Put some cotton swabs aside in the medicine chest. Get the name of a vet that handles birds from the pet shop or call around and inquire. A good bird vet to use is one who sees many birds, not just an occasional one. Put the doctor's name and phone number in your address book for use in an emergency.

Do not panic if your parrot injures itself. Cool thinking is important to prevent further complications. Birds can injure themselves during taming or while left at liberty in the house. They

may fly into windows or mirrors, or have fights with other family pets. You may even come home to find the bird snagged in a toy or the cage door if it tries to break out.

In emergencies, you must act first and then call the vet for follow-up care. If the bird has its leg or wing twisted in the cage on a toy or a string from its cover, approach the bird slowly. Don't frighten it. Speak softly to the bird and untangle the limb or cut the string that is holding it. Remove the bird from the cage and examine the limb. You may have to wrap the bird in a towel or hold it still.

If the limb is bleeding, clean with hydrogen peroxide and see how much damage there is. If minor, you can dress with bird salve and return the bird to its cage. Keep the parrot warm and quiet and observe. If there is a severe wound, stop the bleeding and call the vet for advice.

When your parrot breaks a blood feather badly enough, it will bleed from the broken spot. If the blood drips very slowly, leave the parrot where it is and wait a few minutes. If bleeding does not stop you will have to apply styptic powder. Wait five to ten minutes for the bleeding to stop by itself before taking and medicating the bird. If bleeding is very rapid, do not wait that long. You may have to use pressure in addition to the styptic powder. Press against the bleeding spot with clean dry cotton

and hold for a few minutes until bleeding stops. Place the bird back in its cage and keep it quiet. You will have to see the vet or an experienced bird handler if you think that the feather needs to be extracted. Do not attempt to pull broken blood feathers by yourself if you have no experience. You may cause more harm than good.

Treat bleeding claws or cracked beaks with styptic powder and pressure. Stop the bleeding, if it doesn't stop by itself, and then put the bird back in its cage for rest. If the beak is cracked, remove the bird's water overnight and replace the next morning.

Broken legs and wings should be treated by the vet. Most of the time it is better not to splint or bind the limb. Bandages bother parrots and are usually pulled off in a short time. Remove the perches and the swing from the cage. Place one perch low to the cage bottom and place feed and water within easy reach. Broken limbs will mend in a few weeks if the bird's activity is restricted. Leave the bird in its cage throughout the recovery period. Keep it warm and partially covered. If a broken bone cuts through the flesh, contact your vet immediately. Wrap the parrot in a towel or place it in a small box to immobilize it until you get to the vet.

Whenever a parrot is injured, treat the injury and keep the bird warm and quiet until you can get further advice from an

A pair of healthy Amazon parrots. As soon as it has been determined that a bird is ill, it must be removed from the presence of other birds and its cage thoroughly cleaned.

experienced professional. Don't drag the bird over to the vet without calling first.

It is easier to take a few precautions against common injuries than to treat them once the bird gets hurt. Keep dangling toys and strings out of the cage. Keep sharp objects away from the parrot. Make sure that bells have secure clappers that won't come loose. Pad the floor that the bird could hit if the wing is badly clipped.

ILLNESS

Most Amazon parrots are hardy birds if given a proper diet, enough exercise and protection from drafts. Make a daily check on the parrot's droppings when you feed and clean. The droppings are the most reliable indices of good health. Healthy droppings have good form; they are dark green in color and contain a small amount of white matter. If you notice that the droppings change color to orange, yellow, lime green, or all-

Left: *A tame Amazon enjoys sitting on its trainer's shoulder.* **Below:** *A successful feat in training—the bird sits upon the hand of its trainer.* **Opposite:** *Close contact with any parrot is risky, no matter how tame the bird is.*

white, look for other signs of illness. Watery droppings should also cue you to look for additional symptoms.

Check the amount of seed that your parrot eats when you change the feed dish. If the bird has not eaten what it normally does, see the vet. Birds lose weight rapidly when they don't eat, so learn to keep an eye on the bird's daily intake. Loss of appetite is an indication of illness. Other symptoms to watch for are droopiness, listlessness and fluffed-up feathers. Discharges from the eyes or nose are real problems. Whenever your active parrot suddenly has a change of behavior, examine it and check to see whether it has good weight. If the parrot is thin, see the vet immediately, especially if there are other symptoms.

Sinusitis is characterized by swollen eyes and runny noses. If treated promptly, the condition can be eradicated. If left untreated, sinusitis can develop into serious respiratory illness. Many bird owners are deceived into thinking that sinusitis is not a problem worth treating because the bird does not have a constant discharge from the nose. The illness often bothers the bird most in the morning, and for the rest of the day no discharge is apparent. Sinus trouble should be treated with antibiotic drugs that only your vet can prescribe.

Respiratory colds can begin as simple sniffles and end up killing the parrot. If the Amazon sneezes constantly and shows other symptoms of illness such as red eyes, lack of appetite, or discharge from the nose, keep it very warm until you can get to the vet. A temperature of 90 to 95 degrees will give the parrot the best chance of pulling through respiratory illness. Don't try to treat respiratory colds with over-the-counter medications unless you are willing to gamble with the life of your pet. The vet will probably prescribe antibiotic drugs to treat the cold. It is your responsibility to administer the medications as ordered. Respiratory illnesses include bacterial and viral pneumonia, asthma, aspergillosis, chronic wheezing and coughing, to name a few. All can be treated with the right kind and dosage of antibiotic drugs. Medication alone is not enough to cure these illnesses, however. Heat is very important for combating illness, as is good quality feed and plenty of it.

Digestive disorders can accompany respiratory ills or appear by themselves. Constipation can be treated with mild doses of a laxative. Constipation is characterized by all-white fecal matter or no fecal matter at all. If the bird does not pass any droppings for 24 hours, discontinue the laxative and see the vet immediately.

Diarrhea is most often a

A healthy Amazon parrot will have bright, beautiful plumage, as does the bird shown here. The plumage of a young bird may not, however, be as shiny as that of an adult.

symptom of some other illness. If the parrot suddenly develops very loose watery droppings of a bad color, check the diet and limit the amount of fruit given until the condition is gone. Your vet can prescribe a few different binding medications. If the diarrhea is not severe, the pet shop may have an adequate nonprescription medication. Don't let diarrhea drag on for days if the non-prescription aids don't do the trick. See the vet for chronic diarrhea.

If you ever notice blood in the fecal matter, your bird may have enteritis. This condition must be treated as soon as it is detected. Simple enteritis can become very serious and eventually cause death if left untreated. Take a sample of the bloody stool to the vet along with the bird. The doctor will want to examine the specimen under the microscope to help him determine the problem.

Tumors can appear anywhere on the parrot's body. Most tumors

Above: *Stephen M. Duncan, experienced Amazon trainer, demonstrates the tamability and cooperation that any trainer can accomplish with consistent, patient taming methods.* **Opposite:** *This expert trainer feels confident in allowing his bird to kiss him, but this is not a recommended practice for the inexperienced.*

are not cancerous and can be removed by the vet.

Sinus lumps are often mistaken for tumors. If you think that your parrot has a tumor, don't write it off as dead but see the vet for proper diagnosis and treatment.

Lameness, arthritis, and rheumatoid conditions affect parrots just as they affect people. Legs and feet can become hot and swollen or stiff and sore. The parrot will appear to favor one leg and keep its weight on the other foot. You can treat lameness by holding the affected limb under warm, running water and then painting with a bird salve. If the bird continues to favor the foot, take it to the vet. Lameness and arthritis can develop if the parrot is forced to stand on perches that are either damp or of too small a diameter. Birds that remain outdoors all year round may develop these conditions as a result of exposure to the elements. Poor diet is another contributing factor. Avoid lameness and arthritis by feeding the bird properly and giving it dry perches of adequate diameter. Outdoor birds must be protected from the elements by shelters adjoining their flights.

Going light refers to the bird losing weight for no apparent reason. The torso wastes away and the bird shrivels up. Sometimes there is no cure for going light, but most of the time it is an indication of some other,

treatable disorder. Check the diet and adjust it to give the bird more fattening foods. Ask the vet for appetite stimulants. Have the vet examine the parrot; he may need a fresh stool sample for examination. The parrot may be suffering from internal parasites. The vet can eradicate these parasites with proper medication.

Nervous system disorders may be characterized by the bird losing its equilibrium and constantly falling off the perch. Some birds may lose the power to flap their wings or hold up their heads. Nervous system disorders are not common and may result from past head injuries. See the vet for proper diagnosis and treatment.

Unusually heavy molt can result from either constant overheating or an improper diet. Check the diet and be certain to give the recommended supplements. Adjust the diet when necessary.

Concussion and shock are very serious conditions which usually result from traumatic injury. A parrot in shock does not focus the eyes and does not fight you if you try to pick it up. Breathing is shallow and slow. The bird's feet may be very cold. Some birds emit a soft crying noise with each breath. If your Amazon goes into shock, wrap it up in a towel and heat it up to about 95 degrees. Place it in a small box to keep it still and warm. Don't try to force food or water down its throat or it may choke. Keep an eye on the

The beak and feet of the Amazon parrot are important indicators of good health.

bird, but don't keep unwrapping it to see how it is. The less you move it the better. The bird should recover in a short time. If not, you may have to suspect internal injuries. Keep the bird very warm and quiet and hope for the best. When shock is the result of an external injury, use your discretion. If the wound or injury is severe, treat it first and then treat the shock. If the injury is secondary to the shock, treat the shock first. Shock is often the immediate cause of death with birds, so learn to recognize the symptoms and treat the condition.

Whatever the illness or injury, keep your parrot very warm at 90 to 95 degrees. Keep the temperature constant and activity around the cage to a minimum. In an emergency, act first, then call the vet for follow-up care. By keeping the cage clean and the bird well-fed you can prevent serious illness. Learn to keep a daily check on the bird's droppings and its food intake. When you notice sudden changes in its mood or normal activities, watch more closely for other signs of ill health. Learn to know what is normal for your bird and you will be able to catch illness in its earliest stages. When you seek advice from a qualified veterinarian, listen to what he has to say. If he prescribes medication it is your responsibility to administer it properly.

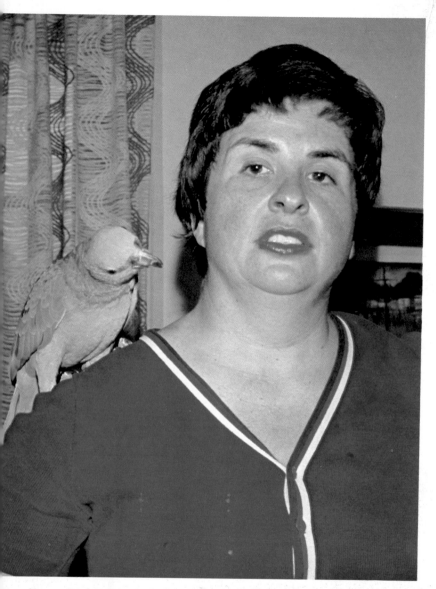

Above: *Amazon parrots are great mimics, and they love to listen to people speak. Pet shop owner Ruth Hanessian is accustomed to having a feathered friend interrupt her conversations.* **Opposite:** *Gentle reassurance helps to build trust between a bird and its trainer.*

Breeding

Although Amazon parrots have been bred in captivity, it is a difficult undertaking. The first problem is properly sexing the birds. The males and females of most species look alike. In some Amazons there are slight sexual differences.

Amazons are not avid breeders in captivity. Sometimes an aviary is fortunate enough to obtain a motivated pair; other times, many disappointing seasons may pass with no live babies.

To successfully breed Amazons, you must provide plenty of flight space. A flight area at least eight feet long is recommended. The nest box can be made of hardwood in the grandfather clock style. Suggested dimensions are 4 to 5 feet deep and 2½ feet wide. The entrance hole should be about 6 inches from the top and 4-6 inches in diameter. Fill the box with wood shavings to within 18 inches of the entrance hole. Staple a strip of wire mesh to the inside of the box to give the hen an easy climb into and out of the box.

The diet should be enriched to prepare the birds to feed babies. In addition to the regular diet, you should begin to feed soaked seed, thoroughly rinsed, to the birds. Give fresh greens in the form of leafy vegetables, like romaine lettuce, turnip tops, carrot tops, spinach, endive, escarole or chicory. Give more fruit than usual as long as the parrots eat it. Be flexible enough to increase or decrease the amount as the birds need. Apples, oranges, peaches, melons, pears, peas, greenbeans, squash, yams and other fruits and vegetables will round out the diet nicely. Sprinkle all soft foods with mineral powder.

Be certain to use the other suggested dietary supplements. Always provide mineral grit and a large aviary mineral block or plenty of cuttlebone. Your birds may even enjoy sod or freshly cut lawn clippings.

Amazons may lay two to four eggs in a clutch, but usually rear only two young. The incubation takes approximately four weeks, but may vary with different species or as a result of the weather. The baby birds fledge out at about eight weeks of age, but again there may be individual rates of maturation according to and within the species. Once the nestlings leave the nest, weaning will take from five to six weeks. The babies are completely independent at approximately 14 weeks of age. In plumage they resemble parents, but are usually lacking the sheen

Opposite: *Breeding Amazon parrots in captivity is a difficult task, especially for the beginner. The first step is to find a compatible breeding pair.*

Left: *After the Amazon accepts your hand, pull your hand slowly toward your body.*
Above: *Allow the bird to sit upon your shoulder.*
Opposite: *The considerable power of a parrot's beak, combined with a sudden scare, could result in injury to an inexperienced handler.*

A rare blue mutation of an Amazon parrot. Mutations do occur in the wild, but because they stand out, they usually do not last long.

of adult plumage. The iris may be darker in color than in adult birds, and the physical size of the babies is slighter than the mature adults.

At 14 weeks the babies can be safely removed from the parents' care and either placed together in a cage or singled out for taming and training. Provide these babies with the same enriched diet that the parents have been getting. By placing them on a seed diet, you can cause them to lose weight and succumb to illness.

Handfeeding baby Amazon parrots successfully has been done by Nita Scheer of Miami, Florida. The formula that she uses contains strained fruits and vegetables, smooth peanut butter, honey, wheat germ and many other ingredients. In South America, the natives feed nest-robbed young on Masa meal, a corn meal product. (See the chapter on handfeeding in Bates and Busenbark's *Parrots and Related Birds* for more detailed information on handrearing formulas and schedules).

Do not allow your Amazon parrots to lay clutch after clutch of unhatched eggs without interruption. This will severely weaken the egg-laying hen. Interrupt the pair from breeding by removing the nest box, but continue to feed the enriched diet. Begin the breeding season by placing the nest box in the flight cage. Allow your parrots two clutches of babies before discouraging further breeding. By allowing them to breed continuously, the babies will become less and less desirable.

If your Amazons hatch young and desert or pick on them, remove them from the nest box and place them in an incubator with a temperature control. Keep the babies at 98 degrees. Feed them on soft formula every two to three hours. You can stretch out the feedings as the babies become older and show that they can take more food in a single feeding. Be careful not to overfeed the chicks or let them become chilled during a feeding. Place them back in the incubator as soon as the feeding is finished.

A FEW ADDITIONAL COMMENTS ON SEXING AMAZONS

Recently, two new techniques for sexing parrots have become

Before allowing any birds to mate, it must be determined that both are in excellent health.

Opposite: *A gentle tap on the beak and a firm "NO" will best stop a parrot that wants to bite.* **Above:** *Never strike a bird; giving love and attention is a much better way to eliminate aggressive behavior.*

Breeding

popular with aviculturists. Both will be discussed briefly. The first is sexing with the use of an endoscope.

This is a minor surgical procedure that can be performed only by experienced veterinarians. A small incision is made on the side of the bird below the abdomen. An endoscope is inserted through the incision. The vet can then look through the instrument, which has its own source of light, and clearly see the sexual organs. This is a sure test of sexuality, but as with all surgical

procedures, some risk is involved.

The second method of determining sex is fecal sampling. Samples of the birds' droppings are collected for laboratory analysis. The samples are examined for hormone and steroid content and then compared to the hormone and steroid content in the feces of known males and females of the same species. This type of testing is not as absolute in its findings as the surgical method, but it in no way endangers the birds.

Amazon parrots make wonderful pets, as long as they are given clean surroundings, nutritious food, and a lot of love and attention.

Index

Finsch's Amazon in an aviary. Finsch's Amazon is rarely found in captivity.

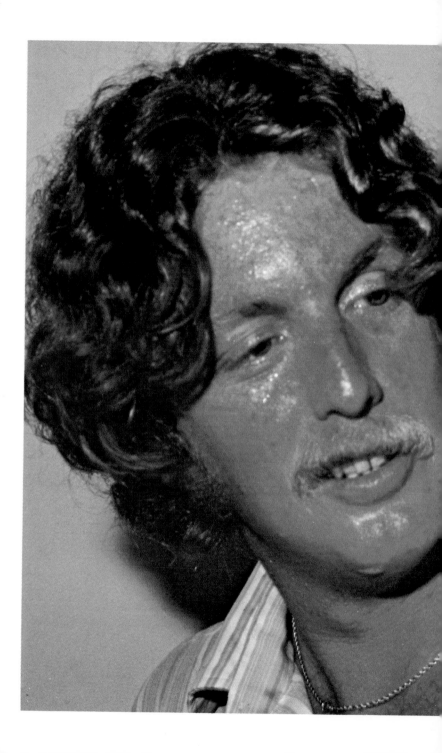

Stephen M. Duncan, experienced bird trainer, with one of his tame Amazons.

TAMING AND TRAINING AMAZON PARROTS
KW-039